FUN WITH THE FLUTE

By William Bay

Online Audio   www.melbay.com/93274EB

• •

First Track for each song contains Flute with Piano accompaniment.
Second Track for each song contains Piano accompaniment only.

AUDIO CONTENTS

• •

Recorded: June-August 2005, White Concert Hall, Washburn University, Topeka, KS 66621
Arranger: Jean Marshall, Adjunct Instructor of Music, Washburn University
Flutist: Amy O. Puderbaugh
Pianist: Rebecca Bumgarner
Producer: Rebecca Meador, Assistant Professor of Flute, Washburn University
Recording Engineer: Lyle Waring, Systems Technician, Washburn University

1 2 3 4 5 6 7 8 9 0

Visit us on the Web at www.melbay.com — E-mail us at email@melbay.com

FLUTE FINGERING CHART

CAMPTOWN RACES

Moderately

Stephen Foster

4

When The Saints Go Marching In

Brightly

Traditional

Moderately

FRANKIE AND JOHNNY

Traditional

Black Is The Color Of My True Love's Hair

Slowly

Folk Song

BLOW THE MAN DOWN

Moderately

Sea Chanty

Michael Row The Boat Ashore

Moderately

Spiritual

RED RIVER VALLEY

Slowly

Cowboy Song

Drink To Me Only With Thine Eyes

Slowly

Traditional

TOM DOOLEY

Moderately

Folk Song

ALOUETTE

Brightly

French Song

AURA LEE

STREETS OF LAREDO

OH! SUSANNA

American Folk Song

Blue Bells Of Scotland

Scotch Folk Song

Look Down That Lonely Road

Spiritual

MY BONNIE

The Eyes Of Texas

Brightly

Traditional

THE ERIE CANAL

Brightly

Traditional

I've Been Working On The Railroad

COCKLES AND MUSSELS

Moderately

Folk Song

Chorus

rit.

LOCH LOMOND

Moderately

Scotch Song

HOME ON THE RANGE

Moderately

Cowboy Song

GREENSLEEVES

Slowly

Old English Song

HATIKVOH
(THE HOPE)

Moderately

Hebrew National Anthem

GYPSY LAMENT

Slowly

Gypsy Folk Song

Bill Bailey Won't You Please Come Home

Bright, With A Beat

Dixieland

Battle Hymn Of The Republic

Julia Ward Howe

Moderately

SHORTNIN' BREAD

Moderately

Traditional

COME BACK TO TORINO

Francesco Carlo Zucco

Bright Waltz

Swing Low, Sweet Chariot

Slowly

Spiritual

SANTA LUCIA

Slowly

Neapolitan Song

LONDONDERRY AIR

Slowly

Traditional

ritard.

Down By The Riverside

With a strong beat

Traditional

Fine

Chorus

D. C. al Fine

Hail Hail The Gang's All Here

Moderately

Traditional

DIXIE

Traditional

Brightly

When Johnny Comes Marching Home

Moderately

Traditional

THIS TRAIN

Brightly

Spiritual

THE DRUNKEN SAILOR

Brightly

Sea Chanty

Chorus

I GAVE MY LOVE A CHERRY

Slowly

Folk Song

SHENANDOAH

Slowly

Folk Song

CAPE COD CHANTY

Brightly

Sea Chanty

Chorus

JOHN HENRY

Brightly

Folk Song

Old Shoe Boots And Leggins

Brightly

Traditional

It Takes A Worried Man

Brightly

Folk Song

THE ENTERTAINER THEME

Scott Joplin